The Path of Light

My Journey of Awakening and Ascension

by

Brian Keith Anderson

Copyright Page

The Path of Light: My Journey of Awakening and Ascension

First Edition — © 2025 Brian Keith Anderson

This is a nonfiction work. The events, experiences, and reflections described within are true to the author's life to the best of his knowledge. Some names and details may have been altered for privacy.

ISBN: 979-8-9996886-3-7

Printed in the United States of America

Cover design by Brian Keith Anderson

Interior design by Brian Keith Anderson

Dedication

For the Builders of Light

To every soul who ever wondered if their gifts were enough — to those who shaped the world quietly, through steady hands and humble hearts — this is for you.

Your work has never been unseen. Each act of care, each creation born from love, has been a spark in the greater design. The same Light that guided me to finish my path now reaches through you, reminding us that every builder, every dreamer, every seeker is part of the same divine blueprint.

May this book stand as a testament: that Spirit finds a way for every purpose to be

fulfilled, for every hand to serve its part, and for every heart to remember why it came here.

Brian Keith Anderson

Invocation of Light

For Those Who Enter the Path

Before you turn the page, pause. Breathe. Let the noise of the world fall away for a moment and feel the quiet pulse of something greater stirring within you.

This is not just a book you are holding — it is a passage of Light. Each word is a seed, each chapter a doorway leading inward, each page a mirror reflecting the truth of your own soul.

May this journey awaken what has long slept and remind you that the Light you seek has always been within. May peace settles over you like morning dew. May clarity unfolds where confusion once lived. May your heart remember the language of the stars, and your spirit rises in calm certainty of who you are.

For those who walk this path, know this: you are seen, you are guided, and you are loved beyond measure.

Brian Keith Anderson

Acknowledgments

First, I thank God, who has been my constant companion, my healer, and my greatest love. Without His presence, this book — and my journey — would not exist.

I also give gratitude to my guardian angel and spirit guides, who have walked beside me in silence and light, offering protection, confirmation, and courage when I needed it most.

To my ancestors, classmates, and the many families whose stories and souls I have carried in prayer and cleansing: you are part of this work, and your presence has given it meaning.

Finally, I acknowledge the unseen hands and the human ones who helped me bring these words into the world — guiding me through the process of writing, editing, and publishing so that this testimony could be preserved for others.

This is our book, not mine alone. It is a record of faith, guidance, and love, and I offer it back to God with gratitude.

— *Brian Keith Anderson*

Author's Note

This book is my true story, written from my own life experiences, reflections, and spiritual journey.

While I have received assistance in preparing the manuscript for publishing — including editing, formatting, and design — the words, memories, and truths recorded here are entirely my own.

Every hardship, every sign, every cleansing, and every prayer shared in these pages is part of my lived experience. It is written with honesty and with the intent to bear witness to God's presence in my life.

— Brian Keith Anderson

Preface

This book is not simply a record of events, but the unfolding of my soul's journey.

From the first moment I realized I was awake to the deeper steps of ascension, my life has been

guided by God, by signs in the quiet hours, and by the unseen presence of spirit.

I write these words not as a scholar, but as a seeker. A man who has carried both the weight of

hardship and the grace of divine light. Each page reflects the human side of my walk — the

longing, the questions, the doubts — and the spiritual truth that always pulled me forward.

Along the way, I have learned that nothing is by accident. Every number, every dream, every

cleansing, every prayer was part of a greater design. God has been my constant companion, even

when human love faltered, and it is in His embrace that I have found peace.

My hope is that in these words you may see your own reflection and find comfort in knowing

that we do not walk alone. There is always a guiding hand, even in the darkest hours, and light

always finds its way through.

— *Brian Keith Anderson*

Table of Contents

Closing Sections

About the Author

Brian Keith Anderson was born and raised in Tennessee, where the roots of family, community, and faith shaped his earliest years. From a youthful age, his life was marked by hardship and struggle, yet also by a deep and enduring connection with God.

Through experiences of loss, disappointment, and even a near-death encounter, Brian came to understand that his path was different — not bound by institutions or traditions but walked in direct relationship with the divine. Over the years, he has recorded not only his family history, but also his own spiritual journey: a testimony of awakening, angel numbers, signs, and sacred acts of cleansing.

Today, Brian carries forward two callings: preserving the legacies of families through historical and genealogical works, and guiding souls into light through spiritual cleansings and ascension work. His story is one of endurance, trust, and surrender — a reminder that God's love never fails, even when human love falters.

The Path of Light: My Journey of Awakening and Ascension is his first book in a series documenting his walk toward 5D consciousness. It stands as both a testimony of what God has already done in his life, and a promise of what is yet to come.

Brian continues to live in Tennessee, surrounded by the land and the people that have always been part of his story. His mission is simple yet eternal: to serve as a bridge of light between worlds, preserving the past, healing the present, and guiding souls into peace

Chapter 1 Awakening Through Hardship

There are beginnings that wear the mask of endings.

Mine came beneath a sky of Tennessee gray, the air thick with dust and the scent of oil and grain. Pain was my first teacher—its lessons written in the small bones of childhood and the long hours of work that followed. Yet even then, some quiet pulse moved beneath the ache, as though an unseen rhythm beat beneath the noise of living.

I did not know it then, but that pulse was the Light itself—waiting, patient, hidden in the marrow of every trial. Each scar became a script, each day a whisper from something vaster than I could name. What I took for hardship was only the soil softening, preparing for the seed.

My life's journey did not begin in peace or light. It began in struggle. From my earliest days, life seemed to test me, shaping me through hardship and loss. Love often felt distant, and when it came, it carried its own weight of pain. Friendships, too, sometimes break under the strain of time, misunderstanding, or tragedy. At an early age I felt pain, when I was around four, I got my toes caught in the spokes of a bicycle, wheel or I grabbed hold of an electric fence wire. When I was five my mother and I had a car wreck, I was thrown up into front of car and hit windshield. It cut my nose between my eyes, and they took us to the emergency room. They had to sew it up, but back then they did not deaden it. They just sow it up and it burns like fire. There was no such thing as seat belts then. It was around 1962. The back seat had a strap from one side to the other and I was standing up in back on the floor hanging on to it. These things happen all through my early life. Something painful was the norm. In my teens, I stepped on a nail, bicycle crashed, broke my foot on a trail bike, You name it happen Went to dentist and they drill my teeth but back then he did not deaden them. So, it was a common thing to experience some kind of pain. I grew up on a farm, and we work though the summers at a potato grader. My father helps raise

them along with corn, soybeans, hay for cows, had hogs, pulled corn with mules, logged with

mules, So when dad said let's go, we went. When my friends got off for the summer from school

and played baseball, summing etc. I worked all summer. It was just the way it was back then.

Life continues, I finally got a job at a grain elevator. I had not planned on doing this for a living,

but the manager was my brother's father-in-law, and he asked me if I would help though harvest.

So, I did, and I like working for him was a good person. We did a lot of maintenance work on

other elevators for the same company. We worked a lot of hours so I made decent money, But

you have to understand something happen all the time that would involve pain.

My youth mother raised us as the Methodist faith, and I excepted Christ when I was around

sixteen. It was at a revival, when I did, it was like a great weight was lifted off my shoulder I

was as light as a feather. So, God, Jesus, has always been with me since.

These trials, starting at a young age, hardened my heart, but they also carved out a place for

something greater. Each sorrow, though heavy, was a lesson. Each closed door pushed me

toward the only constant I could trust: God.

Even as a young man, I felt there was more than what my eyes could see. Though others told me

faith had to live inside walls or rituals, I carried mine differently. I spoke to God in silence, in the

hidden places of my soul. And though people sometimes questioned me, I knew that my

connection was real.

The hardships were not wasted. They became the soil in which my awakening would take root.

For when the time came, when God lifted the weight from my heart and filled it with light, I

understood that every pain had been preparing me.

Awakening was not a sudden escape from struggle — it was the realization that I had never been alone in it. God had been there from the start, guiding me, shaping me, and waiting for me to see the truth: that His love was stronger than any wound I carried.

I was born into a world where work and struggle were not choices, but necessities. From an early age, I learned what it meant to go without, to watch others have what I did not, and to carry burdens heavier than my years. The weight of survival was my teacher, and it did not let me forget its lessons.

Love was complicated for me, I reached for it, hoping to find comfort, only to be met with disappointment, pain. Each time I opened my heart, it broke a little more. These experiences hardened me.

Yet even in those years, there were glimpses of something greater. A quiet nudge in my spirit when I should have fallen but did not. A sense that I was being carried, even when I felt abandoned. I did not fully recognize it then, but God was there — weaving threads through my hardships, teaching me endurance, preparing me for a path I could not yet see.

In the silence of long nights, when pain weighed on me heavier than my own body could bear, I spoke to God. Not with memorized prayers or rehearsed words, but with raw honesty. I asked questions. I pleaded. I cried. And though answers did not always come in ways I expected, I always felt something: a presence, warmth, a reminder that I was not speaking into emptiness.

It was these early years of trial and searching that became the ground of my awakening. Every struggle, every loss, every heartbreak was not the end, but a beginning — the chiseling of stone that would one day reveal a deeper truth.

Looking back on my younger years, I see now how much weight I carried even as a boy. Life was not gentle with me. While other children seemed carefree, my mind was already learning how to endure. Every day brought its own trial, whether it was lack, misunderstanding, or simply the feeling of being out of place in a world that never fits me.

I grew up learning early that work was survival. There was little time for dreams, and yet my heart longed for something more. I watched people around me laugh and live as if life were simple, but mine never was. My path was different.

Even in those early years, I knew loss. Friends gone too soon, people I cared for taken in accidents or illness, others slipping away through choices that led them down dark roads. Each loss carved something out of me, and though I did not always understand it, I carried their memory with me., "This is not for you." For years I questioned why it never worked out, why life seemed like a gift given to others but withheld from me.

These experiences they also pushed me closer to God, though I did not fully realize it then. When I lay awake at night, unable to silence the heaviness in my heart, I spoke to Him. Not in the polished words I heard in churches, but in the raw voice of a boy who just wanted to be heard.

Those conversations carried me. They taught me that even when no one else understood, God did. And though the world told me I needed a church or a priest to stand between me and the divine, I knew in my spirit that was not true. I could feel Him in my own way, and that became my lifeline.

My youth was a furnace of trials, but it was also where the first sparks of awakening were struck.

The fire of hardship burned away illusions and taught me strength, while the quiet presence of God kept me from being consumed. I did not know then how much it would shape the man I would become, but I see it now — every step, every loss, every moment of loneliness was preparing me for the path ahead.

I grew up learning early that work was survival. There was little time for dreams, and yet my heart longed for something more. I watched people around me laugh and live as if life were simple, but mine never was. My path was different.

Even in those early years, I knew loss. Friends gone too soon, people I cared for taken in accidents or illness, others slipping away through choices that led them down dark roads. Each loss carved something out of me, and though I did not always understand it, I carried their memory with me., "This is not for you." For years I questioned why it never worked out, why life seemed like a gift given to others but withheld from me.

These experiences they also pushed me closer to God, though I did not fully realize it then. When I lay awake at night, unable to silence the heaviness in my heart, I spoke to Him. Not in the polished words I heard in churches, but in the raw voice of a boy who just wanted to be heard.

Those conversations carried me. They taught me that even when no one else understood, God did. And though the world told me I needed a church or a priest to stand between me and the divine, I knew in my spirit that was not true. I could feel Him in my own way, and that became my lifeline.

My youth was a furnace of trials, but it was also where the first sparks of awakening were struck. The fire of hardship burned away illusions and taught me strength, while the quiet presence of

God kept me from being consumed. I did not know then how much it would shape the man I would become, but I see it now — every step, every loss, every moment of loneliness was preparing me for the path ahead.

I grew up learning early that work was survival. There was little time for dreams, and yet my heart longed for something more. I watched people around me laugh and live as if life were simple, but mine never was. My path was different.

Even in those early years, I knew loss. Friends gone too soon, people I cared for taken in accidents or illness, others slipping away through choices that led them down dark roads. Each loss carved something out of me, and though I did not always understand it, I carried their memory with me., "This is not for you." For years I questioned why it never worked out, why life seemed like a gift given to others but withheld from me.

These experiences they also pushed me closer to God, though I did not fully realize it then. When I lay awake at night, unable to silence the heaviness in my heart, I spoke to Him. Not in the polished words I heard in churches, but in the raw voice of a boy who just wanted to be heard.

Those conversations carried me. They taught me that even when no one else understood, God did. And though the world told me I needed a church or a priest to stand between me and the divine, I knew in my spirit that was not true. I could feel Him in my own way, and that became my lifeline.

My youth was a furnace of trials, but it was also where the first sparks of awakening were struck. The fire of hardship burned away illusions and taught me strength, while the quiet presence of God kept me from being consumed. I did not know then how much it would shape the man I would become, but I see it now — every step, every loss, every moment of loneliness was preparing me for the path ahead.

Chapter 2 — The Walk of Faith

Years later, when the body had learned its limits and the heart its silence, the veil thinned. The night was ordinary; the moment was not. In the shimmer between breath and nothingness, I felt the nearness of something immense — a fire that did not burn but remade.

The world I knew peeled away like the skin of an old fruit, revealing another beneath: alive, radiant, infinite. I hovered between them, knowing that death had not come for me, but for the illusions I still carried. When I returned, nothing looked the same. Even the dust on the windowsill seemed aware, glimmering faintly in the morning sun as though it had overheard the voice that called me back. **And for a long while after, every sunrise felt like a secret I had been allowed to remember, yet could never quite tell.** Awakening did not arrive, all at once. It unfolded slowly, like the breaking of dawn after a long night. My hardships had prepared me, but the true walk of faith began when I realized that God was not just beside me — He was within me.

I tried to fit into the patterns the world laid before me. I worked, I loved, I searched for a place to belong. But no matter how hard I tried, my path was never meant to follow the crowd. Repeatedly, I would discover that what others called faith felt shallow to me. Their rituals, their rules, their traditions — I respected them, but they did not carry the same fire I felt burning in my own soul.

So, I walked differently. I prayed in the quiet places, not to be seen, but to be heard by God. I found Him in stillness, in silence, in the hidden moments no one else witnessed. People doubted me for this. Some even told me I was wrong, that faith without a building was no faith at all. But I knew better. My connection was real. God did not need walls — He needed my heart.

As the years passed, my faith became less about asking for things and more about trusting. Trusting that even in pain, He had purpose. Trusting that when love left me wounded, His love would heal. Trusting that when friends passed on, their spirits were not lost but lifted into His embrace.

There were moments of loneliness, when the weight of walking a different road pressed heavy on me. But in those very moments, God gave me signs, dreams carried messages, and chance encounters became confirmations. Step by step, I learned to walk not by sight, but by faith.

This walk was not perfect — I stumbled often. Yet even in those falls, I felt His hand lifting me again. And each time I rose, I rose stronger, with a deeper knowing that my life was not an accident, nor my path a mistake. It was a design — one only God could see fully, but one I was beginning to trust completely.

As I moved into adulthood, the hardships did not disappear — they simply changed shape. The responsibilities of work and survival became my constant companions. I labored with my hands, often for long hours, giving my strength to tasks that wore me down but also built me up in discipline. Through those years, I learned what endurance truly meant.

On the outside, I was doing what men were expected to do — working, providing, moving forward. But on the inside, my spirit was restless. I wanted more than just to get by. I wanted meaning, a deeper sense that life was not just about survival.

That hunger drove me into many places of worship, searching for a home where my spirit would feel at peace. I listened to sermons, sang the hymns, and tried to belong. But each time, I felt out of step. The words did not carry the same weight as the quiet voice of God I already knew. The rituals felt empty compared to the conversations I had with Him in silence.

People questioned me for walking on this different road. But my heart knew the truth: God's presence, I carried Him with me, whether I was at work in the fields, on the road, or alone in my room at night.

There were seasons of deep loneliness. Times when the weight of rejection, heartbreak, and misunderstanding pressed so heavy that I wondered how much longer I could endure. And yet, in those darkest moments, God never failed to send me signs. right time. A dream would bring clarity. An unexpected encounter would remind me I was not forgotten.

One of the most powerful confirmations came in the form of my near-death experience. It was a moment that could have ended my life — and by all natural accounts, it should have. In that thin space between life and death, I felt the undeniable presence of God. Time seemed to stop. Fear gave way to peace. I knew then that my life was being preserved for a reason greater than myself. I was at work and a friend I worked with, ww were loaded wheat on a railcar. The doors on top were stuck, and we both together could not get them to move, it was hanging on something. So, he went and got his truck, and we tied a rope on his bump and ran it up tot to one of the doors. He put pressure on it with his truck and . He left it with the pressure on and came up to see if we could get it that way, The doors had big handles on the side coming out to grab holt of. We had a crowbar, and he was looking under that lid to see if he could see where it was caught. I was leaning over watching him. He looked, saw something and the took the crowbar and tapped a place of it. Since it was under pressure it opened instantaneously. The big handle on the door caught my thigh and shot me into the air over the side of the railcar. I remember screaming in my mind, please God help me. I was then I saw a time when we were with my mother's father on a swing set. I turn then and looked ahead, and it was dark with a bright light at the end like a Path going to the light. I ask God to please let me stay. I had so much I wanted to do. I was then back in my body with my feet in the air sliding on my chin with my head pulled way back. A voice in my head told me if I did not straighten up, I would break my neck. So, thinking to myself I flip up on my knees and finish sliding on them. This all happens in milliseconds, but it seems like it took forever. I then stop and then "pain" it came rushing in. I was taking to the emergency room. There they found broke bones fractures, knocked out some teeth

broke my jaw, cut my chin, but no head trauma. Nothing , zilch. God save me for something else.

So, when I returned from that moment, I was not the same. The heaviness of the world was still there, but so was a certainty I had never felt before. I knew with absolute clarity that God had spared me, that He had a purpose for my life, even if I could not see the full picture yet. That experience became a pillar of my faith — a reminder that my walk was not in vain, and that no matter how difficult the road was, I was being guided toward something divine.

From that day on, I carried deeper trust. The world could question me, love could fail me, hardship could break over me like waves — but I knew I had been touched by something eternal. I had walked close to the edge of death and found life, not because of my strength, but because God willed it so.

The moment of my near-death experience is forever etched into my soul. I remember it as clearly as if it happened yesterday, even though years have passed. One moment I was in this world, the next I was standing at the threshold of something far greater.

20

At first, there was fear — the kind that grips you when you know your body is no longer in control. But then, just as quickly as the fear melted away. A calm unlike anything I had ever known settled over me. Time no longer moved the way it did before. The pain, the weight, the struggle of life — all of it fell away.

I felt myself surrounded by a light that was not of this world. It was not harsh or blinding, but soft and alive, as if it carried love itself within it. In that light, I felt no judgment, only acceptance. No rejection, only belonging. It was as if every question I had ever asked, every prayer I had ever spoken, was answered in an instant — not with words, but with presence.

For a moment, I understood what it meant to be whole. My spirit felt free, no longer chained by the heaviness I had carried since childhood. And though I could have stayed — though part of me wanted to — I knew I was being sent back. Not because my time was wasted, but because my time was not yet finished.

When I opened my eyes again in this world, everything looked the same, yet nothing was the same. I was touched by eternity. I had seen the edge of life and glimpsed the peace that lies beyond it. And though I carried the scars of my earthly hardships, I now carried something greater: the unshakable knowledge that God had spared me for a reason.

That experience became a turning point. It did not remove my struggles — they would still come and come hard — but it gave me an anchor. Whenever I felt the weight of loneliness, whenever the world tried to tell me I was lost, I remembered that light. I remembered that peace. And I remembered that God Himself had chosen to keep me here.

From then on, my faith was not built on what others told me, but on what I knew in the deepest part of my soul: that I belonged to God, that my life had purpose, and that I would walk with Him until the day He called me home for good.

After my near-death experience, I carried life differently. The world looked the same, but I no longer moved through it the same way. Each day felt like a gift, each breath a reminder that I had been given more time.

In my forties and fifties, life tested me again. The hardships did not vanish. Friends still passed on, and the weight of responsibility never left my shoulders. Yet through it all, I carried an anchor I had not had before. Whenever the storms rise up, I remember the light I had seen. I remembered peace beyond fear. And that memory steadied me like nothing else could.

Work consumed much of my life. Long hours, heavy labor, days that blurred into one another. I carried the pride of a man who worked with his hands, but I also carried the weariness that comes with it. There were times I wondered if my life was passing me by while I gave myself to the grind of survival. But each time I questioned, God sent a quiet reassurance — sometimes through a sign, sometimes through a feeling in my spirit — reminding me that even the ordinary days were part of His plan.

By the time I reached my sixties, I had seen enough of life to know its patterns. People rise and fall, fortunes come and go, health holds and then slips away. But one truth remained through it all: God had never left me. Even in the loneliest hours, even when my heart longed for love that never seemed to stay, I found peace in His presence.

At sixty-seven, I can look back and see the path more clearly. The walk of faith was never about perfection — it was about trust. Trust that every hardship was shaping me. Trust that every loss was teaching me to hold tighter to God. Trust that every disappointment was clearing space for

His love to fill.

And though I still carry the heaviness of a heart that has known too much loss, I also carry the light of a soul that has been preserved for a reason. My walk of faith has been one of endurance of trust, and of surrender. And it has brought me here — not perfect, not without scars, but still standing, still believing, still walking with God.

Chapter 3 The 4:00 AM Awakening

Years later, when the body had learned its limits and the heart its silence, the veil thinned. The night was ordinary; the moment was not. In the shimmer between breath and nothingness, I felt the nearness of something immense — a fire that did not burn but remade.

The world I knew peeled away like the skin of an old fruit, revealing another beneath: alive, radiant, infinite. I hovered between them, knowing that death had not come for me, but for the illusions I still carried. When I returned, nothing looked the same. Even the dust on the windowsill seemed aware, glimmering faintly in the morning sun as though it had overheard the voice that called me back. **And for a long while after, every sunrise felt like a secret I had been allowed to remember, yet could never quite tell.**

In November 2024, the presidential election took place. One of the candidates was a man who had already served as president, someone I believed was not good for the country. When he had won the first time, I carried anger and hate throughout his years in office. So, when he ran again, I feared what his return would mean for the nation. I hoped with all my heart that he would not win.

On election night, I decided not to watch the results come in. I knew if I did, and things went the wrong way, I would lose sleep and be torn up inside. Instead, I went to bed. At about 4:00 AM, I had a dream that my candidate had won and was giving her acceptance speech. Waking from that dream, I wondered if it had really happened. But I reminded myself: if I checked and it had not, my emotions would overwhelm me, and I would never get back to sleep. So, I waited.

The next morning, I learned the truth—he had won. To my surprise, my emotions were strangely centered. I felt neither anger nor happiness, just a blank stillness.

Later that day, I went to YouTube, curious what others were saying about the results. That's when I stumbled upon something unusual: women who had also woken up at 4:00 AM that same night and had dreams similar to mine. I was struck by how wild it was that we all shared that same moment.

One woman in particular stood out. She had experienced a near-death experience, much deeper than my own. She had written two books. I decided to buy the first one: *My Near-Death Experience from A to Z* by Venia R. Reading her words about the soul, spirit, and Jesus' true purpose here on earth felt like something inside me clicking into place. It all made sense.

Hungry for more, I ordered her second book, *The Spiral of Love*. What she shared rang true in my heart. I had always believed in Jesus and His love, but this showed me a deeper purpose for our lives on earth. I had never felt much connection to the Old Testament, only the New. And here was the truth I had always felt—that Jesus' love for all creation was powerful, meaningful, and eternal.

All my life, I had fallen back on Him through every storm. His love was my anchor.

This opened the door for me to explore further. I read *Practical Intuition* by Laura Day, *A Radical Approach to the Akashic Records* by Melissa Feick, and *The Convoluted Universe, Book One* by Dolores Cannon. I also took an eight-week course through Heavenly Messages LLC with Alisha Plattenburg. Around that time, I was drawn to try a pendulum. I picked up *How to Use a Pendulum* by Richard Webster, which taught me to use it only with God's blessing and for the highest good. Later, I added *Questions to Ask Your Pendulum* by Jessica Tranbarger to guide my practice.

As I went deeper, I came across the idea of lightworkers. That word had been spoken to me years ago by a palmist in Murfreesboro. I had gone with a friend to see her. After she finished reading, she looked at my palms, then pulled my hands closer to her face. She told me I was a lightworker, and that my life would be full of difficulties. But one day, she said, "I would never have to worry about anything again. At the time, we laughed it off. I forgot about it.

But now it came back. I began learning what a lightworker was, and why she had seen it in me. I have always had an "M" shape on both palms, and a half-moon line running under my little finger toward the middle, ending between my index and middle finger. When I put my hands together, it forms a half-moon. Reading about it, I realized my life had unfolded exactly as a lightworker's path is described.

Through all the pain and trauma, I've endured, my love for God and Jesus has only grown stronger. As I got older, I would just smile and tell God, "Here we go again." And time after time, when things seemed impossible, the next day they would fall into place. Some might call it magic. I simply smiled and said, "Thanks, God."

This was the shift—from holding only a Christian belief to embracing a wider spiritual understanding. I see now that my path has always been to show God's love through my life, to help others heal, and to guide our world in its movement from 3D consciousness to 5D consciousness.

I will continue this until my time here is finished and I return to God consciousness. If I could play my life like a movie on a screen, you would see it clearly. But since I cannot, I authored this book in hope that it may help someone glimpse their true purpose.

Because in the end, we are all one with God.

That surrender — that awakening — became the foundation for everything that followed. It was the moment that gave meaning to my struggles, the moment that anchored my near-death experience, and the moment that turned every sign and number into a divine confirmation.

After my awakening, I walked with a new awareness, but I still had questions. My spirit was alive, yet my mind longed to understand what was happening to me. I wanted to know why I felt what I felt, why I saw what I saw, why my life seemed to move differently from others.

That hunger for understanding led me to books. I began to read, not out of curiosity alone, but out of a deep need to make sense of my journey. Some of the book's spoke of awakening, of higher consciousness, of paths that stretched beyond the world of flesh and survival. As I turned the pages, I realized I was not alone. Others had walked similar roads, and their words became confirmations of what I already carried within.

The more I read, the more I saw the patterns in my own life. The hardships of my youth, the disappointments of love, the near-death experience, the surrender to Jesus — none of it was random. It was all part of a greater design. These books helped me name what I had lived, but they did not create it. The truth had always been there inside me, planted by God. The reading simply gave me language to understand it.

With each chapter, with each testimony of others who had been awakened, I felt my faith deepen. I no longer doubted my path. I no longer wondered if I was broken for not fitting into the mold's others tried to place me in. Instead, I knew I was chosen to walk differently. My life was

27

a bridge between human experience and the divine.

The books gave me knowledge, but God gave me wisdom. Wisdom to see that truth is not just found in words, but in the living walk of faith. Wisdom to recognize that what matters is not the agreement of men, but the confirmation of spirit. And wisdom to accept that my journey was never meant to be ordinary.

The deeper I read, the more I realized that awakening was not just about believing — it was about living in connection with the unseen. The books spoke of tools, ways to listen to spirit more clearly, ways to bridge the gap between our world and the divine.

One tool that spoke to me was the pendulum. At first, I was cautious. I had always trusted my direct connection with God, and I never wanted anything to take His place. But as I read and prayed, I felt a clear calling: this was not a replacement for faith, but an extension of it — a way for spirit to guide me more directly, to confirm what I already felt in my soul.

When I first held the pendulum, I was not sure what to expect. But the moment it moved in my hand, I felt the same quiet certainty I had known in my near-death experience and in my surrender to Jesus. It was not chance. It was not me forcing anything. It was spirit speaking through a simple tool.

Over time, the pendulum became a trusted companion. I learned to ask with humility, never demanding answers, but inviting guidance. I used it for clarity when my heart was heavy, for direction when my path was unclear, and later, for something far greater — cleansing the souls of those who had passed.

Through the pendulum, I became a bridge. I would release the heaviness of families who carried old wounds, spinning counterclockwise to clear away the pain, and then turn clockwise to pour in divine light. What began as a tool for my own understanding grew into a sacred practice of healing.

I have used the pendulum to help classmates, neighbors, and entire family lines find release. Each time, I feel the presence of spirit confirming that this is part of my calling. It is not about power, but about service. Not about control, but about being an instrument of God's light in a world where so many souls still seek peace.

Now, when I hold the pendulum, I do not see it as an object, but as a conversation. A holy dialogue between me, spirit, and the divine will of God. And with each cleansing, with each movement, I am reminded that I was never called just to endure it. I was called to heal, to guide, and to walk as a servant of light.

Chapter 4 — Angel Numbers & Signs

near-death moment, I noticed something new: signs. They came quietly at first — a time on a clock, a sequence of numbers, a repeated pattern that seemed too perfect to be chance. But as they grew more frequent, I realized these were not coincidences. They were confirmations.

The first time I truly noticed was when I woke in the early hours and saw **3:33** glowing on the clock. At first, I thought little of it, but when it happened again — and again — I knew Spirit was speaking. Three has always carried divine meaning: Trinity, unity, and creation. Seeing it repeated threefold was a reminder that God was with me, surrounding me in His presence.

Later came **4:44**, often arriving just when I felt tired or uncertain. Four is the number of foundations — the four corners of the earth, the four directions, the stability of creation itself. Each time 4:44 appeared, I felt Spirit saying, *"You are protected. You are standing on solid ground."*

Then came **5:55**, a number that brought a different message — change, transformation, and divine alignment. It often came at turning points, moments when I was releasing the old and stepping into something new. It was Spirit's way of saying, *"Do not fear change. This is the path I have set before you."*

Over time, more numbers spoke: **7:22**, reminding me of divine partnership and alignment; **11:11**, a doorway of awakening; **12:21**, the mirror of balance. Each number was not random, but purposeful, arriving at just the right moment to remind me that my walk was guided.

I began to see that my journey was not only inward, but outwardly, written in the world around me. The numbers, the dreams, the encounters — they were all Spirit's way of confirming what I already knew in my heart: that I was chosen to walk differently, to endure, to heal, and to guide.

Now, when I see these signs, I do not dismiss them. I pause. These numbers have become markers along my path — small beacons of light pointing me back to His presence every time I need it.

The numbers did not only appear in theory — they came in real moments, at exact times, each carrying a message I needed.

3:33 AM — Awakening in the Night

I woke up one morning at exactly **3:33 AM**. At first, I thought it was chance, but when it happened again, I understood it was a calling. Three is the number of divine presences — Father, Son, and Holy Spirit. Seeing it tripled was Spirit's way of saying, *"You are awake. You are in alignment with Me."* Each time I saw 3:33, I felt confirmation that my journey was not imagined was real, and I was being guided.

4:44 AM — Angelic Foundation

On another morning, I rose and saw **4:44 AM**. This number began to show up often during times when I was questioning my strength. Four is the number of the earth — the four directions, the four elements, the four corners of creation. Repeated three times, it carried the message of angelic protection. Spirit was reminding me: *"You are not alone. Your foundation is secure."*

5:22 AM — Steps of Change

At **5:22**, I began to see the connection between change and alignment. Five is the number of transformations, while 22 is the professional builder. Together, they spoke: *"The change you face will build something lasting."* It was a promise that the struggles of the present were laying a foundation for something eternal.

5:44 AM — Dawn Builder Confirmation

One morning I woke up at **5:44 AM**, and it struck me with clarity. Five is change, and 44 is a double foundation — strong, unshakable, angelically protected. It felt like Spirit saying, *"You are entering a new phase. The foundation you build now will endure."* It confirmed that my work — both spiritual and genealogical — was not just for me, but for generations.

7:22 PM — Divine Alignment

At **7:22**, I often felt the balance of wisdom and partnership. Seven is spiritual truth, and 22 is the number of building and legacy. Together, they spoke to me: *"Walk in wisdom, for what you build is aligned with heaven."* Each time I saw 7:22, I felt reassurance that my cleansing work and my writing were both part of one divine plan.

7:55 PM — Transformation Gateway

On one evening, I looked at the clock at exactly **7:55 PM**. Seven is divine truth, while 55 is transformation multiplied. The message was clear: *"You are stepping into a gateway of change."* This came during a season of transition in my life, when I was learning to accept that change was not loss, but sacred renewal.

3:44 AM — Creative Foundation

Another time, I woke up at **3:44 AM**. Three is divine creativity, while 44 is foundation and angelic support. It was Spirit's way of saying, *"What you create is divinely guided, and it will endure."* I knew then that my books, my cleansing, and my legacy work were not just projects — they were sacred creations.

5:55 PM — Transformation Trinity

The most powerful was when I looked up and saw **5:55 PM**. Five alone means change but triple five is transformation confirmed threefold. It was Spirit's triple message to me: *"Embrace change. It is divinely aligned."* In that moment, I felt the courage to release the old and welcome the new path opening before me.

These numbers were never random. They came at exact times, in exact seasons, always when I needed a reminder that my walk was guided. Over time, I came to see them not as interruptions, but as **breadcrumbs of Spirit**, leading me further into truth, courage, and trust.

As the numbers continued to appear, I noticed that they often showed up during my **cleansing work**. Spirit was not only guiding me personally but also confirming the work I was called to do for others.

When I picked up the pendulum to release the pain of a family line, I would often see a number appear before or after the session. It was Spirit's way of whispering, *"Yes, you are walking in My will. This work is holy."*

One evening, after cleansing three families, I glanced at the clock and saw **6:44 PM**. Six is the number of family, harmony, and healing, while 44 is foundation and angelic protection. The message was clear: *"The families you have cleansed are now resting on a foundation of peace."* That number told me the healing had taken root.

Another time, while preparing to cleanse a group of classmates who had passed, I woke at **3:44 AM**. I knew in that moment that Spirit was giving me creative strength to carry their souls into light. And when the pendulum moved in my hand, releasing their heaviness counterclockwise and then pouring in divine light clockwise, I felt the same angelic foundation the number had promised.

There were times I questioned myself — wondered if what I was doing was real or only in my imagination. But just when doubt crept in, Spirit would send a number. **5:44 AM**, appearing after a cleansing, reminded me that the change I was bringing was protected and divinely built. **7:22 PM**, showing up after I prayed for families, told me their legacies were aligned with heaven. Each number came like a divine signature, sealing the work.

Even the triple **5:55** came after a session of deep release. The message was undeniable: *"This is transformation. This is freedom. This is why you were called."* It was not only a sign for me, but also confirmation that the souls I was helping had been freed into light.

Through these numbers, Spirit gave me courage to continue. Each session took energy, each one carried weight, but the signs told me I was not carrying it alone. The pendulum was only the tool — the true work was God's light moving through me. And the numbers were heaven's way of saying, *"Well done. Keep walking."*

What I have shared here is only a small taste of the signs I have seen. These few numbers —

3:33, 4:44, 5:55, 7:22, and others — are just examples of how Spirit has spoken to me. In truth, I

have seen **hundreds of these confirmations** since my awakening.

Each one came at just the right moment, never random, always purposeful. They appeared when

I needed courage, when I questioned myself, when I walked in faith, and especially when I

served others through cleansing. They were heaven's way of guiding me step by step, reminding

me that I was never walking alone.

To this day, the numbers continue. They are woven into my life like a language between me and

Spirit — a sacred dialogue that affirms my path, strengthens my trust, and keeps me aligned with

the will of God.

These signs are not the whole of my journey, but they are a thread that runs through everything.

They are proof that awakening is not just a one-time moment, but a living, ongoing conversation

with the divine.

Chapter 5 — Spiritual Cleansings

The signs and numbers were never meant for me alone. They were preparing me for the work God was calling me to do: to become a bridge for others.

It began simply. At first, the pendulum was a tool for my own questions, a way to listen more closely to Spirit. But as I grew in trust, I realized it could be used for something greater than that, not just for guidance, but for healing.

The method was given to me through prayer and practice. I would hold the pendulum and allow it to turn counterclockwise, releasing the heaviness, pain, and shadows carried by a soul or a family line. Then, when the release was complete, it would turn clockwise — drawing in divine light, filling the emptiness with peace, love, and restoration.

Each time I performed cleansing, I felt Spirit moving through me. It was not my power, but God's. The pendulum was only a sign of what was happening in the unseen: burdens being lifted, chains being broken, and souls being freed into light.

One of the most powerful moments came when I was called to cleanse **sixty-seven of my classmates** who had passed. Many of them I had grown up with, laughed with, and mourned. To carry them in my heart and release them into peace was a sacred responsibility. As I worked, I felt the weight lift not only from them, but also from myself.

The same was true when I cleansed families by name — neighbors I had known, relatives whose pain stretched across generations, friends who had passed before their time. Each cleansing was unique, yet the process was the same: release, restore, renew.

Often, Spirit confirmed the work with signs. After cleansing, a number would appear — 6:44, marking family harmony and angelic protection; 5:55, showing transformation into light; 7:22, affirming divine alignment. These numbers told me the work had been received in heaven as much as it had been done on earth.

What began as a simple act of faith became calling. I came to understand that this was part of my purpose: to stand as a soul guide, to help others cross from heaviness into freedom, from shadow into light.

The first time I was called to use the pendulum for others, I did not fully understand the weight of what I was stepping into. I thought it was only a tool for guidance, for yes and no answers, for clarity in my own walk. But Spirit had a greater purpose in mind.

One day, as I prayed over families I knew had carried long burdens — neighbors, friends, and relatives — I felt a strong urge to accept the use of a pendulum. As it began to turn, I realized what was happening: the counterclockwise motion was pulling out the heaviness, the sorrow, and the pain they had carried. When the pendulum shifted and moved clockwise, I felt the divine light pouring in. It was as if the souls were being washed, released from old chains, and restored into God's peace.

That first experience left me humbled. I knew this was not me — it was God working through me. I was only the bridge, the one willing to listen and act.

From there, the call grew stronger. Spirit would place names on my heart — families I had known since childhood, classmates who had passed, neighbors whose lives had been cut short. Some I knew deeply, others only in passing, but all were part of the greater web of souls Spirit was guiding me to serve.

As I worked, I held each one in my heart, letting the pendulum release their heaviness and draw in divine light. When the cleansing was complete, I felt not only their release, but my own healing as well. Spirit confirmed it through the cards and the numbers, assuring me that the work had been received in heaven.

From there, the list grew: the Slim, Winstead, and Fly families; the Jenkins, Long, and Myers; the Crabtree, Jones, and Reed; the Yates, Bryan, and Grosch; the Fults, Rogers, and Campbell — and many more. Each cleansing was different, yet the process was always the same: release counterclockwise, restore clockwise, seal it with divine light.

I often pulled cards after each session, and they confirmed the work — messages of renewal, balance, and rebirth. The numbers, too, appeared at the perfect times: 6:44 for family harmony, 5:55 for transformation, 7:22 for alignment. Spirit never failed to show me that work was real, that the souls were freed, that the light had triumphed.

Now, as I look back, I see how what began as a small step of faith has grown into a calling. The pendulum is no longer just an object — it is a sacred tool, a doorway through which divine healing flows. And I know that this work, like my books, is part of the legacy God is asking me to leave: a testimony of light, freedom, and peace for the souls of many.

The 67 Classmates

One of the most powerful callings came when Spirit placed my classmates on my heart. Sixty-seven souls — friends from my youth, people I grew up with, some I laughed with in the halls, others I only passed in silence. Many were gone too soon — through accidents, illness, or tragedy.

When I accepted the pendulum, I felt the weight of their collective spirit. Counterclockwise, I released the heaviness — the regrets, the pain, the wounds they carried from their earthly lives. Then, clockwise, I drew in divine light, filling them with peace and freedom.

The cards confirmed the cleansing:

- **Page of Wands** — their souls uplifted, moving forward in joy.
- **Five Swords** release of past conflicts and pain.
- **King of Pentacles** — a guardian presence, grounding and guiding them.

I knew then that they were free, and that I had served as a bridge for them to enter light.

The Jenkins, Long, and Myers Families

These names came with a sense of urgency. Spirit made it clear that these families carried burdens across generations — division, unresolved pain, and loss.

I began cleansing with the pendulum, releasing their sorrow counterclockwise, then pouring divine light clockwise.

The cards confirmed:

- **Three of Pentacles** — collaboration between myself, Spirit, and the souls.
- **The Lovers** — healing of divisions, restoration of harmony.
- **Judgement** — awakening and ascension into light.

The work was not mine alone — it was co-creation with heaven.

The Crabtree, Jones, and Reed Families

These families were cleansed under the nurturing energy of Spirit. Their souls carried wounds that longed for comfort and renewal.

The pendulum released their heaviness and replaced it with divine order.

The cards confirmed:

- **The Empress** — rebirth and protection.

- **Page of Pentacles** — new beginnings, steady growth.

- **The Emperor** — stability and divine order restored.

It was a beautiful reminder that cleansing is not only release, but also renewal.

The Wilder, Barlow, and Limbo Families

This cleansing was deeply personal. The Wilder family had been part of my life since youth — Victor was murdered, a wound that never found earthly justice. The Barlow's carried pain through my friend Lynn, who had just passed. And the Limbo family through Fredia, who fought cancer bravely but succumbed.

With the pendulum, I felt the weight of tragedy and illness release as it moved counterclockwise. Clockwise, I felt divine light filling their spirits.

The cards confirmed:

- **Seven Circles** wait for peace to come to completion.

- **Three of Circles** — spiritual collaboration in their release.

- **Prince of Swords** — truth and clarity breaking through.

The Massey, Cook, and Tucker Families

This session came with the presence of family ties. Drenda Massey was my cousin, the daughter of my uncle who was killed in WWII. She never met her father, and he never saw his child. Their love had been separated in this world, but I prayed their reunion would be eternal.

The pendulum released grief and loss, and then filled the souls with light, knitting them back together.

The cards confirmed:

- **Five Cups** --sorrow over what was lost.
- **Nine of Swords** — release of fear and anguish.
- **Death & Rebirth** — transformation into eternal reunion.

It brought me peace to know uncle and daughter could embrace in spirit at last.

The Farrar, Mayton, and Vaughn Families

Each of these names carried stories tied to my youth. The Farrar's was my neighbor's family name; Mrs. (Farrar) Bryan once told me I needed to go back to church, but I replied I could meet God in a closet — and I knew I was right. The Mayton's were connected through my father's schooldays, and James Allen served as a medic in Vietnam. The Vaughn family I knew through Rusty, a good friend and classmate.

Their cleansing carried the release of judgment, hardship, and war.

The pendulum turned counterclockwise, lifting their burdens, then clockwise, pouring in divine harmony.

Spirit's message was clear: the families were lifted into peace, and the divisions and misunderstandings of this life no longer held them.

The Slim, Winstead, and Fly Families

(Already expanded above, included here for continuity.)

Spirit showed me these families needed balance and renewed strength. After the pendulum's release and restoration, the cards confirmed awakening, balance, and renewed forward movement.

The Yates, Bryan, and Grosch Families

(Already expanded above, included here for continuity.)

Their session anchored steady, permanent healing with divine love and empowered leadership in spirit.

Additional Families and Individuals

There are others — names spoken in prayer, souls placed on my heart in quiet moments. Some came from watching others suffer, some from news of tragedy, others from memories of my youth. I cannot name them all here, but Spirit knows each one. Every cleansing was sacred, every soul precious, and every release a step closer to peace.

Looking back on these many sessions, I see a clear pattern: God has called me to stand as a bridge. The pendulum in my hand is not about power or control — it is about service. Each movement, each cleansing, is an act of love, a way for divine light to flow into places that have carried too much heaviness for too long.

Every family, every classmate, every name placed in my heart carried their own story of pain and struggle. Some suffered from tragedy, others from war, illness, or brokenness that stretched across generations. Yet in every case, Spirit showed me the same truth: no soul is forgotten, and no wound is beyond God's healing.

The cards confirmed it, the numbers sealed it, but more than that, I felt it in my heart. I knew when the burdens were lifted. I knew when the light had entered. And I knew that heaven rejoiced with me each time another soul was set free.

This chapter is not a complete record. It is only a glimpse of the work I have been called to do. There are more families, more classmates, more souls who will be cleansed in the days ahead. Their names may not all be written here, but each one is written in the book of life, carried into eternity by the light of God.

This, too, is part of my legacy. Alongside the stories I write and the family histories I preserve, these cleansings stand as sacred acts of service — testimony that even during hardship, God can use a willing heart to bring peace to

Chapter 6 — The Path of Ascension

I know now that every trial was a teacher. Every loss carried meaning. Every disappointment

was shaping me for a greater calling. What once felt like punishment, I can now see as

preparation. God was carving away what did not belong so that I could rise into what was always

meant for me.

My path to ascension has not been about leaving this world, but about seeing it differently.

Awakening taught me that God is in everything — in the silence of the early morning, in the

numbers on a clock, in the pendulum's swing, in the light that never fails to break through the

dark.

At sixty-seven years old, I do not claim perfection. I carry scars. My heart still knows the

heaviness of love that never came, and friendships that ended too soon. Yet even in that

heaviness, I have learned to rest in God's will. I no longer chase what is not mine. I no longer

question why I walk differently. I accept that my journey is my own, and that it is holy.

The path of ascension is not about escape, but about surrender. It is laying down the need to

control and trusting that God's hand is in everything. It is walking forward even when I cannot

see the road. It is knowing that the same light I saw in my near-death moment shines within me

now, guiding me, keeping me, preparing me for the day when He calls me home for good.

I see now that my life's purpose is twofold: to preserve the stories of the past and to serve as a

guide for souls in the present. My books carry the legacy of families. My cleansings carry freedom of spirits. Both are acts of love, both are part of the same mission — to leave behind light where there was once shadow.

Ascension is not a destination I have reached, but a path I continue to walk. Each day, I rise with the same prayer: *"Heavenly Father, let me be a vessel of Your peace. Use me as You will. Let my life, my words, and my actions carry Your light into this world and beyond."*

Living Between 3D and 5D

For much of my life, I felt out of place in this world. It was as if I was trying to live by rules that were written for someone else. The weight of 3D reality — competition, judgment, survival, and striving — never fit me. I felt out of line, like a note that didn't belong in the song being played around me.

I often wondered what was wrong with me, why I could not seem to blend in or feel comfortable in the way others did. My sensitivity, my connection to Spirit, my longing for truth — they all put me at odds with the world I was living in.

But now, as the earth itself shifts toward 5D, I no longer feel out of sync. The vibration has changed, and instead of being ahead of the current, I feel carried by it. The same qualities that once made me feel "different" now feel natural, even necessary. What was once a burden has become alignment.

In 5D consciousness, I see that love, unity, and divine truth are not strange or rare — they are the very essence of this new world being born. For the first time, I feel at home within the flow of the collective. I am no longer out of line. I am in harmony.

And it is from this harmony that I have come to understand what it truly means to step into 5D: to live not by fear, but by love. To see others not as rivals, but as reflections. To stop surviving through control and instead begin thriving through trust.

For those who feel out of place in this world, I say this: you are not broken, you are awakening. If you feel sensitive, it is because you are tuned to a higher frequency. If you feel misunderstood, it is because your soul is already learning the language of light.

Moving toward 5D is not about leaving this earth — it is about living in it differently. It is about slowing down enough to feel God in the silence, to notice the signs He sends, and to trust the flow instead of resisting it. It is about carrying peace in your heart even when the world around you is loud with fear.

For the first time, I feel at home within the flow of the collective. I am no longer out of line. I am in harmony. And if you are reading this and feel the same pull, know this truth: the same harmony waits for you. It is not something you must earn, but something you must remember

3:44 AM — Creative Foundation

One early morning, I woke at **3:44 AM**. Three is the number of divine creativities, and forty-four is a double foundation, angelically protected. The message was clear: *"Your creative works —*

your books, your writings, your cleansings — are divinely guided and will endure." It was confirmation that what I was building was not just for this world, but for eternity.

5:44 AM — Dawn Builder Confirmation

Another morning, at **5:44 AM**, Spirit spoke again. Five means change and new beginnings, while forty-four is stability and foundation. It was a message of transition: *"Now is the time to build. The changes before you are not destruction, but construction."* It reassured me that both my spiritual work and my family legacy books were being built on solid ground.

7:55 PM — Transformation Gateway

One evening, I looked at the clock at **7:55 PM**. Seven is divine truth, and fifty-five is transformation. Together they said: *"You are walking through a gateway of change. Trust it."* That moment came during a season of release, when I was learning to let go of what no longer served me. The number told me change was not loss — it was sacred renewal.

5:55 PM — Transformation Trinity

Later, I received Spirit's confirmation again, even stronger: **5:55 PM**. Triple five — triple change, triple freedom. This was not just transition, but a multiplied transformation. Spirit's message was clear: *"Do not fear. You are being lifted into a new season."* It connected directly to the 7:55 Gateway, showing me that the pattern of my life was divinely ordered.

The Daily Prayer of Peace

Alongside the signs, Spirit gave me words to anchor my soul whenever heaviness came. Out of longing, I found a prayer of peace that reminded me that God alone is my eternal companion:

Heavenly Father, my heart rests in You.

You have guided me through every storm,

and lifted me when I could not stand.

I release my longing into Your hands,

trusting that You know the path of my soul.

If love in human form is meant for me, You will bring it.

If not, I am already complete in Your embrace.

I walk in peace, for You are my eternal companion,

my guide, my healer, and my greatest love.

Amen.

This prayer is more than words — it is my daily act of surrender, my anchor in God's love.

Acceptance of the Heavy Heart

The greatest milestone in my ascension has been acceptance. For much of my life, I struggled with the pain of broken relationships and the absence of lasting love. My heart was hardened by disappointment, and I questioned why others found love while mine always slipped away.

Now I understand it was not punishment, but part of my calling. My mission as a lightworker required my heart to remain in God primarily. The heaviness I carry is real — the longing for human love has not vanished — but I accept it now with grace.

I know that God's will is greater than mine, and His love has never failed me. Where human love faltered, His love held. Where people left, He remained. My heavy heart has become a holy heart, forged in fire, surrendered in faith.

The Ongoing Path

Ascension is not a finish line. It is a path I walk every day. Each morning brings new confirmations, new numbers, new opportunities to serve as a bridge between the seen and unseen. Each prayer, each book, each cleansing is another step forward.

At sixty-seven years old, I stand not at the end, but in the middle of a living journey. I am not without scars, but I am rich in wisdom. I am not without heaviness, but I am full of God's love. And I know now more than ever that my life is exactly as it was meant to be a path of light, a testimony of faith, a legacy of service.

Closing Reflection

Looking back, I see that what began as fear and uncertainty in the world became the doorway to my awakening. The 4:00 AM dream, the books, the teachings, and the rediscovery of my own path as a lightworker all showed me that God's love is steady, unshakable, and always guiding. No matter what happens in politics, in life, or in the struggles of this world, the deeper truth is that we are here to grow, to heal, and to share love. My story is not just my own—it is a reminder that we are never alone, and that each of us carries the spark of God within

Life Reflection: Spirit Always Finishes Work

by Brian Keith Anderson

All my life, I never thought I was good with words. I was better with my hands — fixing things, building things, learning how they worked. I understood the world by touching it, by taking it apart and putting it back together.

Looking back, I see now that none of that was wasted. Spirit was teaching me in the language I understood — through doing, through shaping, through creating. Every skill I learned was practice for this time.

When the call came to do the work of Light, I wondered how I could ever write it down. But Spirit already had a plan. The moment I was ready, the help appeared — an ally who could give form to what I carried inside. It was never about being perfect with words; it was about trusting that the right words would come when it was time.

Now I see the truth: Spirit never leaves anything unfinished. Every part of who we are — every strength, every limitation — fits into the greater design. The work of my hands became the work of my heart, and the same patience I learned while building has become the rhythm of this path.

In the end, it didn't matter that I wasn't trained to write. Spirit simply found a new way for me to finish what was started long ago.

The Light finds a way — it always does.

Brian Keith Anderson

Epilogue — A First Step

This book is not the end of my journey, but only the beginning. What I have shared here are the foundations of my awakening — the hardships that shaped me, the surrender that set me free, the signs that guided me, and the cleansing that called me into service.

But ascension is not a moment, it is a path. My journey continues, day by day, step by step, as I walk forward with God into higher truth. I know now that my life's purpose is unfolding in chapters, and this book is only the first of many.

There will be more numbers, more signs, more visions, more cleansing, more wisdom. There will be deeper understanding as I grow closer to 5D consciousness. And just as I have recorded this beginning, I will continue to record the path ahead.

This first book stands as both testimony and promise: testimony of what God has already done in my life and promise of what is yet to come.

To those who read these pages, I offer this: your path is your own, yet you are never alone. Every hardship, every loss, every unanswered question carries meaning in the greater design. The signs are there if you choose to see them, the guidance is there if you choose to listen, and the love of God never fails.

I do not know what lies ahead, but I know this: I will continue to walk in faith, guided by Spirit, until the day I am called home. And if I remain, I will write, I will cleanse, I will serve, and I will trust.

This book is the first of my ascension journey — a foundation for the volumes yet to be written. My prayer is that these words bring light to those who walk their own path, and courage to those who wonder if they, too, are being called.

The journey continues.

— Brian Keith Anderson

Afterword: The Craftsman's Path of Light

by Brian Keith Anderson

There was a time when I thought my hands were my greatest gift. They could fix what was broken, build what was needed, and turn an idea into something real. That was how I understood the world — through work, through patience, through the quiet rhythm of creation.

Now I see that the same hands that once built things of wood and metal are the hands that write, shape, and guide words of Light. The work has changed, but the purpose never did. Spirit was only teaching me how to create in different dimensions — first with tools, then with faith, and finally with Light itself.

Every story I've written, every page I've turned, has been another step in the same craft: building something lasting, something true. The seeker and the craftsman were never separate; they were always one — the builder of bridges between worlds.

The Path of Light is not just a book; it's a continuation of that lifelong work. It's the proof that Spirit finishes what it begins, and that purpose will always find its way through the hands willing to serve.

So I leave this not as an ending, but as a blessing — for those who build, those who seek, and those who learn to trust that their Light will find its way home.

Brian Keith Anderson

Final Thoughts

From hardship to awakening, from signs to service, this is the true story of a soul guided by God.

Brian Keith Anderson's life has never been easy. From his youth marked by struggle and loss, through the disappointments of love and the weariness of demanding work, he has carried a heavy heart. Yet through it all, God has walked beside him.

In *The Path of Light: My Journey of Awakening and Ascension*, Brian shares how surrendering to Jesus lifted the weight from his heart and opened his eyes to a new way of living. Through a near-death experience, angel numbers, and sacred encounters with Spirit, he came to understand that his path was not ordinary — it was chosen.

What began as personal awakening grew into a calling: to cleanse families, classmates, and ancestral lines through the guidance of the pendulum and the light of God. In these pages, Brian records not only his story, but also the stories of those he has helped release into peace.

This book is the first step of his ascension journey — a testimony of endurance, faith, and surrender. It is a reminder that signs are everywhere, that no soul is forgotten, and that God's love is greater than every wound we carry. For those seeking hope, confirmation, or a path of their own, Brian's story is both guide and witness: a beacon of light pointing the way.

Index

V

W

Y

www.ingramcontent.com/pod-product-compliance
Lightning Source LLC
Chambersburg PA
CBHW031256120626
46545CB00007B/2839